Crystals Explained

Crystals Overview, Types of Crystals, Uses and Benefits, Cleansing Rituals, Step by Step Guide for Consulting Crystals, and More!

By Riley Star

Copyrights and Trademarks

All rights reserved. No part of this book may be reproduced or transformed in any form or by any means, graphic, electronic, or mechanical, including photocopying, recording, taping, or by any information storage retrieval system, without the written permission of the author.

This publication is Copyright ©2019 NRB Publishing, an imprint. Nevada. All products, graphics, publications, software and services mentioned and recommended in this publication are protected by trademarks. In such instance, all trademarks & copyright belong to the respective owners. For information consult www.NRBpublishing.com

Disclaimer and Legal Notice

This product is not legal, medical, or accounting advice and should not be interpreted in that manner. You need to do your own due-diligence to determine if the content of this product is right for you. While every attempt has been made to verify the information shared in this publication, neither the author, neither publisher, nor the affiliates assume any responsibility for errors, omissions or contrary interpretation of the subject matter herein. Any perceived slights to any specific person(s) or organization(s) are purely unintentional.

We have no control over the nature, content and availability of the web sites listed in this book. The inclusion of any web site links does not necessarily imply a recommendation or endorse the views expressed within them. We take no responsibility for, and will not be liable for, the websites being temporarily unavailable or being removed from the internet.

The accuracy and completeness of information provided herein and opinions stated herein are not guaranteed or warranted to produce any particular results, and the advice and strategies, contained herein may not be suitable for every individual. Neither the author nor the publisher shall be liable for any loss incurred as a consequence of the use and application, directly or indirectly, of any information presented in this work. This publication is designed to provide information in regard to the subject matter covered.

Neither the author nor the publisher assume any responsibility for any errors or omissions, nor do they represent or warrant that the ideas, information, actions, plans, suggestions contained in this book is in all cases accurate. It is the reader's responsibility to find advice before putting anything written in this book into practice. The information in this book is not intended to serve as legal, medical, or accounting advice.

Foreword

Crystals and gemstones are pieces of stone that are both appealing and naturally 'powerful.' This is the reason why these stones are used in making jewelry pieces and worn by men and women alike. But apart from its beauty, these gems are also prize for its natural energetic properties which adds to its aesthetic value. They are naturally powerful in various ways, and it can also bring out confidence and emit beauty to the wearer.

Here's a bit of trivia for beginners like you; crystals came from the molten layer of the Earth, and it rises on the surface through hot gases and mineral solutions. The molten layer will eventually become cool, and the atoms that are contain within it will arrange itself into patterns of 3 – dimensional lattices, once the atoms are aligned and cooled off (crystallization process), the finish product is what we call crystals. Gemstones also go through the same process before transforming into crystals. Keep in mind though that not all crystals are gemstones and not all gemstones go through the crystallization process. For instance, grains of salt and snowflakes are a type of crystals but they didn't go through the crystallization process.

And because of a crystal's special structure, these beautiful stones can then transmit, amplify, and absorb electromagnetic energy which magicians and spiritually inclined individuals tap in order to either energize a person or help heal an illness. You'll also find out that crystals and gemstones also attract positive energy vibes (lucky charms) while some people use it as an amulet because crystals and gemstones are also believed to ward off negative energies and protect a person from bad luck or misfortune. Others simply use it for aesthetic purposes not being fully aware of its magical component.

You will not only learn about the natural properties of crystals and gemstones but also its energetic and magical elements that anyone can harness and use in their daily lives. This book will focus on crystals and gemstones that are from natural rocks, organic materials and minerals like those that are being used in jewelry. You're also going to learn the various types of crystals/ gemstones including their qualities and properties as well as how you can use these magical qualities and apply them into your life. Each of us has a unique connection with these stones, and some are also naturally aligned to their energies. You will get to discover which stones you are most connected with! Are you ready?

Table of Contents

Introduction 1
    Powerful Psychic Energy Tools 2
Chapter One: The Power of Crystals.. 5
    What are the Crystals 6
    The Power of Crystal Magic 7
    Uses of Crystals in Ritual and Magic 9
    Acquiring Crystals and Gems 11
Chapter Two: The Power of Your Intentions 13
    What is an Intention?... 15
    Uses of Crystals 18
Chapter Three: Selecting the Right Crystals 23
    Cleansing and Caring for Your Crystals........................... 26
        Salt Water 27
        Smudging 30
Chapter Four: Other Cleansing Methods for Your Crystals 37
    Other Cleansing Methods 38
        Rain 38
        Rivers or Running Water 40
        Ocean 41
        Sunlight... 44
        Moonlight... 46

Earth or Soil	47
Sea Salt	50
Herbs and Dried Flowers	53
Quartz Crystals	56
Tips When Cleansing Your Gemstones and Crystals	58
Caring Tips for Your Gemstones and Crystals	60
Chapter Five: Crystals and Their Benefits	63
Crystals and their Uses	63
Agate	63
Alexandrite	64
Amber	65
Amethyst	66
Angelite	67
Emerald	68
Fluorite	69
Hematite	70
Howlite	71
Jade	71
Quartz Crystal	72
Rose Quartz	73
Ruby	74
Sapphire	75

Tourmaline 76

Turquoise 76

Aquamarine 78

Aventurine 79

Citrine 79

Garnet 80

Herkimer Diamond.. 81

Chapter Six: Methods and Instructions for Using Crystals . 83

Methods for Attracting Love.. 83

Attracting Someone Who Shares Your Interests 84

How to Draw the Right Lover..................................... 87

How to Invite Love in Your Life by Preparing Yourself Mentally, Emotionally and Physically 89

Attracting New Friendships into Your Life 91

Methods for Attracting Prosperity and Wealth................ 93

Attracting Money and Success.................................... 93

Creating a Financial Lucky Charm............................. 96

How to Ensure That You Always Have the Money You Need 98

Chapter Seven: Other Purposes of Crystals 101

Crystals for Emotional Balance 101

Crystals to Lift Your Spirit... 102

How to Ease Away from Emotional Distress 105

How to Keep Creative Ideas Flowing 108

How to Find Inspiration.. 109

Crystals for Empowering Yourself with Positive Energy 111

Using Crystals to Live Each Day in Happiness 112

Using Crystals to Increase the Flow of Good Luck 115

Cleansing a Room or Space of Negative Energy 115

Improving the Flow of Energy within Your Home 118

Crystals for Protection 118

Photo Credits 121

References 123

Introduction

There are a lot of people who own crystals and gemstones though I bet most of them aren't aware of the true 'power' that these natural elements actually possess. If you take a closer look at the crystals and gemstones you have, you are actually looking at a piece that came from the core of the Earth which is why it contains very powerful energies that are unique and can also be helpful to you in ways you would've never imagined. Learning how to use the energies within these stones can ultimately help you materialize anything that you desire, or perhaps bring you

Introduction

closer to whatever it is you want to manifest in your life. In reality, these crystals have unlimited powers that will help you manifest your dreams, and influence your life for the better. As with anything, the only limit is our imagination.

Powerful Psychic Energy Tools

Why do these crystals and gemstones are being used as powerful energy tools in order to help manifest one's desires? It is because they possess powers or energies that are in alignment on one's psychic level. As you go along in reading this book, you'll learn that working with these stones usually involves psychic/ mental energy. It's all a matter of being aligned and attuned with the energies that the crystals and gemstones possess, and how you care for them will usually come from you inner psychic/ mental reserves.

The unique, powerful, and natural energetic structure of each crystals and gemstones is the reason why it makes an effective psychic/ magical tool. The magical properties that each of these stones possess can be used for various

Introduction

purposes such as protection, healing, manifestation of one's dreams, and empowerment. Believe it or not, these pieces of stone from the center of the earth contains energetic forces that can attract a love life, wealth and money as well as spiritual strength which is why many people always use them as "lucky charms."

Crystals and gemstones actually contain magnetic vibrations that can positively impact the energy that is surrounding them including a person's energy field. And since these stones have its own unique properties and energies, each of them produces a different powerful effect which can then be used for different purposes. Some of these stones can charge you with energy; others attract things, while others can put an individual in a calm and peaceful state which can help a person to experience some sort of greater levels of peace particularly during meditation practices. You'll soon find out that each of the crystals and gemstones radiates different frequencies and levels of energy that's unique to each stone similar to how each of our fingerprints are unique.

Introduction

The powerful energies that these stones contain have been used in many traditions and cultures throughout the ages. They have been used for magical purposes, and have been treasured and collected both as elegant accessories/adornments and powerful energetic qualities.
Learning the amazing powers of these stones can help you manifest your wishes and help fulfill it through knowing its energetic properties and using it appropriately.

The next chapters will teach you how to choose crystals for various purposes, how to clean them, and the powers that each of these crystals and gemstones possess. The more you understand them, the more useful and powerful it will become for you. Keep in mind though that even if these crystals can positively impact and potentially influence your life, you still need to act and put it into good use otherwise it won't work. As what Uncle Ben from Spiderman said, "Great power comes with great responsibility."

Chapter One: The Power of Crystals

If you give crystals a closer look, you'll see that it has many angles, and you'll probably feel that these stones evoke some form of mysterious sense to it. For most magicians, these stones seem to silently evoke the creative, living and infinite power of our planet. Crystals have been revered throughout the ages and it has been used as jewelries and talismans dating back to ancient times. Today, these special minerals are widely used for healing, for enhancing energy in physical spaces, and other variety of magical uses. We will discuss the basic principles of crystal magic in this chapter.

Chapter One: The Power of Crystals

What are the Crystals

"Crystals" in magic and magical circles refers to various types of solid minerals produce naturally from the Earth's ground. Not all of it can be considered true crystals though they still belong in the category of crystal magic.

"Mineral" refers to any inorganic substance that naturally formed through the underground geological working of the Earth. Each mineral is composed of unique and specific chemicals along with its own energy power. The cool thing is that ever since magicians, shamans, healers and witches knew how to use these energetic powers to empower, attract, protect, heal, and influence one's life.

Various minerals have a molecular structure that usually forms a regular pattern. It often creates flat surfaces as well as various geometric forms that shape into a typical crystal we all know of. One of the most popular crystal mineral is the (clear) Quartz. This is the mineral that magicians use as a crystal ball. Other popular crystals include Amethyst, Rose Quartz, Jade, Bloodstone, and Lapis Lazuli among others. These crystals are composed of more than one type of mineral which is why they are not considered true crystals. Amber and Jet crystals shouldn't be classified as one because technically speaking, they are fossilized organic substances and not stones but it's understandable because people in general interchangeably use the words stones and crystals.

The Power of Crystal Magic

For non – magicians crystals and gemstones are classified as inorganic materials but for magicians and spiritual healers they consider these stones to be alive because they believe that crystals impart energy to not just people but also in plants and animals.

Certain types of crystals like the tourmaline and quartz actually exhibit a powerful aspect that they possess, and scientists call it the Piezoelectric Effect. Through experiments, scientists have seen that stones can give off electric charges when mechanical pressure is applied by tapping them using a hammer or through squeezing them.

Chapter One: The Power of Crystals

Quartz and certain crystals also give off pyroelectricity which means that these stones can release an electric charge when they have been exposed to a change in temperature. Only a few types of crystals that are popularly used in healing and magic have shown magical qualities in scientific experiments, and modern science has yet to find out and understood the other healing effects of crystals. One thing is for sure though from a scientific point of view – every crystal emits its own energy that can interacts and affect other energy fields surrounding it; this is perhaps where the "magic" happens.

Magicians understand and knew the power of stones, gemstones and crystals because they believe that the same power that these stones emit is quite similar to the inherent power found in other natural phenomena like the river, and the wind. All matter, visible or invisible, is made up of energy, and all energy is neither created nor destroyed, this is a fact. Energy is interconnected and it can be harnessed through the power of our thoughts or simply intention. It can also be sent out into the cosmos through the energy field of the crystals or gemstones you will choose to use. In this context, gemstones and crystals are conduits of energy. They are tools with specific energy fields that one can use to bring healing and send off positive vibes to the spiritual world in order to manifest one's desire in the physical realm.

Uses of Crystals in Ritual and Magic

In most magical practices, crystals are also used to create a sacred space or circle before a magical ritual starts. During the ancient times, specific crystals are also used to honor gods and goddesses. Some magical tools like pentacles and wands as well as magical jewelries often come with specific crystals and gemstones to evoke certain energies.

In the field of magic, gemstones and crystals are basically used for divination, healing and manifestations of things like wealth and love. They are traditionally used as talismans, lucky charms and amulets, and they can also be powerful tools for spell - work whether as adjunct ingredients or as the main focus of the spell.

Chapter One: The Power of Crystals

For instance, amethyst is usually used to boost power for different spells while clear quartz is usually placed on the altar in order to sharpen focus especially for more complicated spells. However, you can also charge a certain crystal for a specific purpose. For example, citrine can be used to attract wealth, and red jasper is used for courage.

Crystal magic also includes taking advantage of the unique color correspondences in a natural way since they don't have to be dyed like cloth or candles which are also used as magical tools. Colors are vibrations of light, and they resonate with various aspects of life like health, happiness, and wealth depending on their particular vibrations. For instance, the color pink found in rose quartz crystal is an energy that harmonizes with the "love energy" which could make it a great force to attract love into your life. Another example is the color green that's usually found in bloodstone and jade crystals which resonates with abundance and matters of prosperity

Chapter One: The Power of Crystals

Acquiring Crystals and Gems

Gemstones and crystals can be bought in magic shops and even online. There are various stores that also sell specific minerals. However, according to magicians, usually the crystal or stone will be the one to choose you, and not the other way around. You could be given with a crystal from someone you know or even find one in unexpected circumstances like say during a hike or a road trip. Some also buy crystals and gemstones from a trusted supplier, and most magicians say that intention can help one to choose the right supplier and crystals to work with.

You might experience that you are likely drawn to a particular crystal stone, or you may feel that you are sort of being attracted toward a certain type or certain color. This is why most magicians suggest that when you're purchasing crystals or gemstones, you should also take the time to listen to what your body or intuition is trying to tell you. The emotional energy you have will likely be attracted by a certain crystal, so if you feel a positive energy towards a certain stone then you should follow that.

Chapter One: The Power of Crystals

No matter how you get your crystals, you need to make sure that you clean them first "to remove any unwanted energy." You need to prepare your magical tools and charge your crystals with your intentions before you do any spellwork so that you can enjoy the benefits of the energy fields and power that they have.

The next chapter will teach you more about how crystal magic works and it will guide you on how to prepare them.

Chapter Two: The Power of Your Intentions

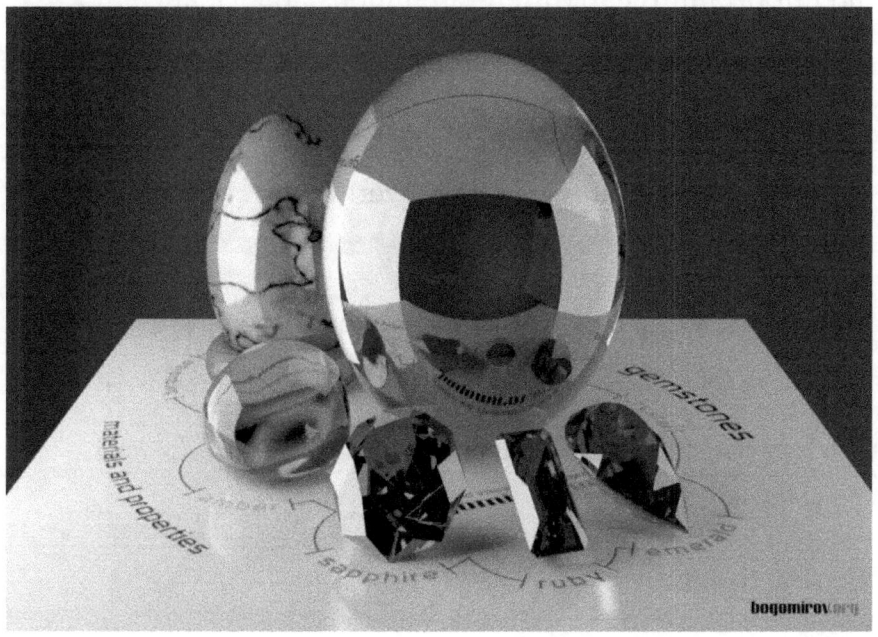

As you now know, gemstones and crystals are unique just like people. Each crystal also gives off specific energy which is why it can be used for various purposes such as spell – casting, magic, and healing. It can also empower, energize, balance, bring peace and uplift an individual. These stones can also lessen stress, promote vivid dreams, balance the energy field in one's space, and enhance learning abilities. Crystal energy can therefore help you in almost any aspect of your life, and different ancient cultures believed that these stones contained an energy force that ancient

Chapter Two: The Power of Your Intentions

people use when conducting rituals and spells. It also played an important role in different religions; in fact, ancient priests believed that these stones are tools that can ward off any evil spirits or forces. Legend has it that the lost city of Atlantis used crystals and its power!

The tomb of Queen Pu – Abi in Sumeria wore ancient pieces of jewelry as found by the archaeologists which dates back to the 3rd millennium B.C. Ancient Egyptians and Indians also used sacred crystal stones for healing and during rituals.

It's not actually necessary for an individual to possess magical abilities for gems and crystals to be effective. In fact, all of us can use the energy that these crystals have through the power of intention and desire which we are all capable of doing. If you want to perform a particular ritual to attract something to your life, you and the crystals/ gemstones will function as a tool/ conduit so that you can be aligned in the energy field of the universe and eventually attract your desires. Crystals can connect you to the infinite power of the cosmos, and you access it through intention.

Chapter Two: The Power of Your Intentions

What is an Intention?

According to scientists and psychologists, our thoughts or intentions create vibrations that are then sends out to the universe. If it is done consistently and properly, setting intentions is a very powerful force for any individual as it can definitely manifest whatever it is that we truly desire – happiness, health, and wealth. If you can align your thoughts or intentions with the frequencies/ vibrations of whatever you want to manifest such as your dreams, values, and aspirations you can then materialize it in the physical world and achieve it (although of course, it should be accompanied with actions).

Setting a purposeful intention can also help you to live in the now, and not be caught too much on negative thought patterns. You see, intentions are like magnets, it can attract anything but it's also a double – edge sword because it doesn't recognize whether a certain thought or intention will be good for you or not. This is why psychologists and physicists believe that one must learn how to think positive thoughts more than negative ones because it can influence

Chapter Two: The Power of Your Intentions

the outcome or the result. Needless to say, your thoughts and intentions attract everything – good and bad.

So, how do you craft a good intention? The tips below can help you align your energy according to your purpose, values, and desires which can be beneficial whenever you're using your crystals and gemstones.

Tip #1: Decide on what is important for you. If you want to find fulfillment in any area of your life, you have to first and foremost decide on what truly matters to you – not to your parents, or friends, or other factors/ people. You need to know what you truly value and be specific about it because if you don't know what you truly value, you'll never be satisfied with anything. Keep in mind that your values drive the actions in your life. For instance, if you value your well – being, your actions will be geared towards your health. If you value money, your actions will be geared towards wealth. If you value love, your actions will be geared towards building relationships, so on and so forth. Of course, you don't have to choose one because obviously there are many aspects of our lives. What is important is you know and choose your values.

Chapter Two: The Power of Your Intentions

Tip #2: Assess your life. If you don't know where to start, or you think that "value" is a big word, what you can do is to simply assess your current life, and see where you need an "upgrade" or perhaps an improvement. Do you want to improve your health life, your relationships, or your financial life? You can focus on one aspect first while trying to find out what you truly want.

Tip #3: Know your What, When, and Why. This is where intention comes in. Once you've already assess your life and the things that are important to you, you must be specific as to what you truly want to achieve along with other details like when you want it to happen, and most importantly your big WHY. The reason why charms don't work sometimes is because people don't know how to set intentions; oftentimes people send out vague messages or energy to the universe and they wonder why their "wishes" didn't come true. Intentions are meant to be intentional. You need to focus your thoughts in something and make it crystal clear, so to speak. For instance, if you want to improve in your finances, you don't just say, "Oh I want to be rich" – that's vague; you have to be specific because the universe will then ask you, rich in what? How much do you want? When do you want it? Why? It's like making an order in a restaurant, you don't just say to the waiter, "I want to order a great dish" then when you do get any dish, you will most likely complain because that's not what you want. It's the same thing with thoughts and intentions. One way of bringing intentions to life is through writing your dreams down in the present tense as if you already have it now, and affirm the things you truly want. Emotional energy is also needed if you want to bring these thoughts to life. It's not enough that you just think about it, you have to feel it! The good thing is that your crystals will also help you bring out such positive emotions and energy.

Uses of Crystals

Energy Attunement

Crystals can make you attune to the natural energy and qualities it possess. You can do this through touching or moving it from hand to hand as you focus on the specific qualities of each crystal or stone. As you do this, you will

Chapter Two: The Power of Your Intentions

notice that there's some sort of tingling or vibration in your hands, this is a sign that you are already consciously aware of the energy being emitted from the crystal. It will then form a "bond" with you.

Amplification of Energy

Each gemstone and crystal already possesses a certain energy that you can work with. If your intention resonates to the natural energy contained in a particular crystal, it will then amplify it. What you can do is hold the crystal using both hands for around 5 minutes as you inhale through your nose, and exhale through your mouth. Doing this can make your intention connect with the innate qualities of the crystal and it also activates and amplify the life energy contained in it.

In addition to this, there are various ways on how to use your crystals; some people place an amethyst crystal under their pillow so that their sleep will be filled with good dreams while others carry it with them every day. You can also place these stones around your plants so that it will grow properly, on the desk at your work so that it can somewhat inspire you, or even put it next to the computer or

Chapter Two: The Power of Your Intentions

laptop so that the electromagnetic energy can be diffused. Many people say that crystals can help one to have a clear mind, and uplift one's spirit. Amulets are believed to repel negative energies and ward off evil. You can also place a crystal at your house as it can also create harmony.

Meditation

Crystals can also be used during meditation. It's important to note that it's best that you work with the same crystal every time you meditate. As mentioned earlier, crystals can attune you and your energy field making you reach in a much deeper meditative state in no time. It can amplify one's intention, thoughts, and will. Once you made the connection to a specific crystal everything will be enhanced. Meditation is an important factor along with a clear mind as it can help achieve great outcome and it's also essential component for healing.

Healing

Crystals and gemstones have been used for millennia by many cultures as part of rituals and ancient/ religious practices. There are no specific rules on how to use it, and

Chapter Two: The Power of Your Intentions

our ancestors most likely just trusted their intuition and work with it in a way that they are comfortable in. The more you use your crystals, the more connected you will be with the particular energy it inherently has.

You will develop your own style as you go along and use each crystal, same with how healers work their own way in using these stones. Appropriate crystals can be placed on an area of the body that needs healing. Keep in mind that gemstones and crystals aren't meant to replace traditional treatment, and it's also not the cure for all illnesses. What it does best is act as a complementary therapy.

You can also use crystal wands to help you become more attuned to the subtle energies that the stones emit. Crystal wands usually have a rounded end, and a pointed end; this can help recharge the body of the afflicted. Healers often hold the crystal and point it to the part of the body that needs healing. You can then visualize white light emanating from the tip and flowing towards the body. It is believed that crystal healing can bring the body into balance and clear internal blockages.

Chapter Two: The Power of Your Intentions

Crystal/ Gemstone Journal

We advised you to keep a journal and record everything you do including the type of crystal or gemstone that you used along with their properties, how you used them, the results, how you felt after using them, and the likes. Keeping a journal will inform you which crystal works best depending on your purpose.

Chapter Three: Selecting the Right Crystals

There are no specific guidelines to follow when selecting crystals or gemstones. Needless to say, just like ancient healers, you just need to trust your instincts because the crystals and gemstones will 'speak' to you, and you'll know intuitively which one suits you.

When choosing a crystal or gems, it's ideal to check out different shops, and revisit them if ever you do not find any stones during your first visit. In addition to that, you can also check out small souvenir or antique shops that specialize in crystals or gemstones. You may also find the right ones through an online supplier, or local stalls nearby.

Chapter Three: Selecting the Right Crystals

The important thing is to keep an open eye especially when you go around because the right crystals are usually found in the most unlikely places. It is believed that the crystals themselves will help you find them as their energies connect with you, and you'll naturally be drawn to them.

Before you search for the right crystals and gems, it's ideal to meditate and set out an intention to find the right stones for you before leaving. You can also visualize yourself holding the crystals as this can help in finding the right ones.

Signs that You've Found the Right Crystal

There are intuitive signs that you have found the right crystal or gemstone to work with. Take note of the following signs or experiences below:

<u>The feeling of being drawn to a specific stone</u>

For instance, if you feel like you just can't take your eyes off of a particular crystal; this is a sign that it is 'calling' you. You may likely be drawn back to it even if you choose to ignore it.

Chapter Three: Selecting the Right Crystals

You may feel a strong nudge or urge that you need to take or buy the stone no matter what

If you feel uncomfortable with the thought of not owning a particular crystal or stone, this is another sign that it's the one for you. There could be lots of crystals and gemstones to choose from but if all of a sudden, a particular stone/ crystal caught your attention, or it stands out from the rest even if it looks so similar. This is another sign that you need to pick it up.

You might also feel a certain kind of energy when you touch a particular crystal or stone.

You will most likely experience such signs and you shouldn't shrug it off or ignore it. The energy of the crystals or gemstones is naturally link to you which is why you should look more intuitively whenever you're selecting a stone. Don't be limited to the signs above because when you find the right crystal/ gemstones, you'll just "know" it. Keep an open heart and mind when searching for the right stone as this can help you in also connecting to the right stone.

Chapter Three: Selecting the Right Crystals

Most importantly, always listen to what your intuition tells you, and you'll never go wrong.

Cleansing and Caring for Your Crystals

Once you've found your crystal and gemstones, the first order of business is to cleanse it. Never ever use a crystal that hasn't been cleansed yet, and do not also place it with your other collections of cleansed stones because it can contaminate the energies of your collection as well as the intention you're trying to set out.

Each crystal and gemstone absorb the energy of whoever handles it which is why it's prudent to cleanse it before you use it so that the energies are purified and neutralized, and also be 100% effective.

There are different ways on how to clean crystals/gemstones. The methods usually involve various tools, materials, locations, and ingredients. Just use whatever method you feel is right. This section will guide you on how to do various types of cleansing, but later in the book, you

Chapter Three: Selecting the Right Crystals

will also learn specific cleansing methods for certain types of stones. For instance, there are crystals that need to be submerged in water, and there are others that should not be submerged. Since there are different crystals and gemstones, it will take time before you learn how to become attuned with it but once you keep on working with them, you'll eventually learn how to use them. It'll become second nature to you the more you use them.

The methods below are the most common ways of cleansing crystals and gemstones:

Salt Water

Most crystals and gemstones can be cleansed with water though common sense will tell you that that's not the way it should be cleaned. It's also best to do this type of cleansing at night especially when you see the moon starting to wane. For crystals that can be submerged in water, make sure to follow the steps below:

Chapter Three: Selecting the Right Crystals

Materials Needed:

- Bowl of warm water. Keep in mind though to never use boiling water when cleaning your stones because it could destroy the qualities of it.
- 1 tablespoon of sea salt
- The crystal/ gemstone

Instructions:

Step #1: Go to a quiet place in your house or in a location where you wouldn't be disturbed. Make sure to bring all the materials with you as you sit down comfortably.

Step #2: Try to relax your body and mind as you close your eyes while taking deep breaths. In order to effectively cleanse the crystal, your own mind and energy should be relaxed and try to get rid of distracting or negative thoughts. Relax your body and don't slouch. Try to empty your mind, and just gently put your thoughts aside.

Step #3: Once you feel relaxed, you can now open your eyes. Take the bowl and place it right in front of you.

Chapter Three: Selecting the Right Crystals

Step #4: Sprinkle the sea salt into the warm water, and as you do this make sure to visualize that the purifying qualities of the salt is cleaning any unwanted energy from the crystal (though don't put the crystal yet). You can also imagine the water becoming more pure than before.

Step #5: After doing step 4, you can now take the crystal that needs to be cleaned and place it in the bowl. Let it submerged in the water for around 10 mins. While waiting, it's best to meditate and imagine the crystal being cleansed. Visualize it being free from all impurities from the surface down to its core.

Step #6: After 10 minutes or so, you can now open your eyes.

Step #7: Take the crystal out of the bowl and rinse it with cool, running water. Make sure to handle your crystal with care as you do this.

Step #8: Once your crystal has been rinsed, you can let it dry outside under the waning moon. If it's possible, it's ideal to let the waning moon shine upon your stone so that the purification process will be more effective. The waning moon is believed to remove any residual energy left in the a crystal making it effective during cleansing.

Chapter Three: Selecting the Right Crystals

Step #9: Retrieve your stone after waking up, and keep it in a safe place.

Smudging

For crystals and stones that can't be submerged in water, you can use a smudge stick for cleansing. A smudge stick is basically a bundle of dried herbs or leaves that's tied together with a string. It's also made up of sage. Some healers use lavender or pine to create a nice scent. The smoke coming from the smudge stick and the purifying properties of the herbs is what cleanses the crystals. This material can be bought in many magic shops, or you can also create one on your own. Here's how:

How to Make a Smudge Stick

Creating a smudge stick that's firmly held together requires practice but it doesn't have to be perfect especially on your first attempt. The most important thing is to keep improving as you go along. Creating your own smudge stick

Chapter Three: Selecting the Right Crystals

can also make you bond more or become more connected to your stones since you're the one who created the tool to clean them. Prepare the materials below:

- A thin and strong piece of string that can tie up the herbs
- Herbs
- Scissors to cut the herbs

Here's a list of herbs you can use for your smudge stick:

- White Sage - this is the most commonly use sage herb when creating a smudge stick. You can still use an ordinary sage and mix it with other herbs like the following:
- Lavender
- Pine
- Cedar
- Mugwort
- Cilantro
- Sweet grass
- Copal
- Juniper

Chapter Three: Selecting the Right Crystals

Instructions:

Step #1: Prepare all your materials and find a quiet place where you cannot be disturb while you're creating your smudge stick.

Step #2: Meditate, close your eyes and visualize for a couple of minutes on the task that you're about to do. Focus on the cleansing properties of the sage and herbs as well as what these can do to cleanse your crystals/ gems.

Step #3: When you're ready, open your eyes and start your task.

Step #4: Take the herbs and cut it into about 6 to 10 inches. Continue cutting until you have enough herbs that have the same length.

Step #5: Place the herbs in one hand and use the string to wind it all up. Start with the base of the herbs, before you work your way up to the tips. Once you get to the tips, start winding it down towards the base.

Step #6: After you wound up the string from top to bottom, the next thing to do is find the other end of the string then tie

Chapter Three: Selecting the Right Crystals

the 2 ends into a knot. Make sure to neatly tie up the herbs but not too tight, cut off any excess.

Step #7: Remove any pieces that are falling off as well as the herbs that are sticking out.

Step #8: Your smudge stick can now be used to cleanse for your crystals and gems.

How to Cleanse Your Stones Using a Smudge Stick

Using a smudge stick in cleaning your crystals is quite hard because it requires a lot of focus. Since you're not physically washing your stones, you need to be mentally connected as you are physically present with the task of smudging. This will make it easy for you to intuitively know when the crystal/ gems have been completely cleansed.

Prepare the following materials before doing your cleansing ritual:

- Your DIY smudge stick
- Candle
- Lighter, match or anything that can light up the candle

Chapter Three: Selecting the Right Crystals

- Fireproof dish
- Crystals, gemstones that needs cleansing

Instructions:

Step #1: Go to a quiet place in your house or in a location where you wouldn't be disturbed. Make sure to bring all the materials with you as you sit down comfortably.

Step #2: Try to relax your body and mind as you close your eyes while taking deep breaths. In order to effectively cleanse the crystal, your own mind and energy should be relaxed and try to get rid of distracting or negative thoughts. Relax your body and don't slouch. Try to empty your mind, and just gently put your thoughts aside.

Step #3: Once you already feel relaxed, you can now open your eyes and light up the candle.

Step #4: Light the smudge stick using the candle flame. It's easier and safer to light the stick this way rather than lighting it directly with a lighter/ match. When lighting the stick, just let it burn until the end becomes red ember before blowing out the flames. The idea is to let the sage smolder

Chapter Three: Selecting the Right Crystals

until it produces smoke because this is how your crystal will be cleansed.

Step #5: Once the stick is already smoking, make sure to place a fireproof dish to catch falling embers and prevent any fire accidents.

Step #6: Once the stick is already producing smoke, you can then move it around the crystal/ gemstones. Let the smoke surround the crystal and just gently fan the smoke with your hand so that the air will be directed to the stone.

Step #7: As you do this, imagine that the herbs are purifying your crystals and the impurities of it are being dissipated with the smoke.

Step #8: Once you feel that the crystal has been cleansed, you can then extinguish the smoke on the smudge stick by running it with water or pushing it in a bowl of sand. Allow it to dry afterwards.

Keep in mind that when you're doing this, make sure that babies, children, pregnant women and people with respiratory illnesses or allergies are not around. Do it in a well – ventilated area if possible.

Chapter Three: Selecting the Right Crystals

Chapter Four: Other Cleansing Methods for Your Crystals

Using the smoke of sage and water submersion are the easiest and most practical methods of cleansing crystals and gemstones. There are still various ways on how you can clean these stones – through nature. Nature offers different means of purification such as the flowing water from the rivers and oceans, soil from the earth, light of the sun and moon among others. You will get to learn the step – by –step

Chapter Four: Other Cleansing Methods for Your Crystals

procedure on how to utilize these natural cleansing methods in this chapter.

Other Cleansing Methods
Rain

Water from the rain can be a great way to clean your crystals and gems. Obviously, you can't do this all the time unless it's consistently raining in your location but if for some reason you predicted the rain right, you can take advantage of it by placing your crystal on the ground where the rain can wash over it.

In order for you to attune yourself with this method of cleansing process, follow the steps below:

Step #1: Once you've place the crystal out in the rain, you can then start meditating at the comfort of your home. Make sure to find a spot where you wouldn't be disturbed, and make sure that your crystals are also in a safe and undisturbed location under the rain.

Chapter Four: Other Cleansing Methods for Your Crystals

Step #2: You can now start relaxing your body and mind by closing your eyes and taking a couple of deep breaths. In order to effectively cleanse the crystal, your own mind and energy should be relaxed and try to get rid of distracting or negative thoughts. Relax your body and don't slouch. Try to empty your mind, and just gently put your thoughts aside.

Step #3: Visualize the rain washing your crystals' impurities. Continue doing this until you feel on an intuitive level that your gems and crystals are thoroughly cleansed.

Step #4: Once you've already felt in you that the crystals and gems are being cleansed, you can now rinse the crystal/ gem and let it dry inside the house.

Step #5: You can also wait until the rain is over or as long as you feel it is necessary for the gems/ crystals to be cleansed before bringing it back inside but just make sure that you don't leave it for a very long time. It's ideal that you bring it back inside as soon as the rain stops, and rinse it.

Chapter Four: Other Cleansing Methods for Your Crystals

Rivers or Running Water

If you live near a river bank, or creeks that have fresh and running water, you can also utilize these bodies of water in cleaning your crystals/ gems. In order for you to attune yourself with this method of cleansing process, follow the steps below:

Step #1: Find a quiet spot by the pond or river where you won't be disturbed. You can then sit down comfortably near the creek or river to prepare yourself for meditation.

Step #2: You can now start relaxing your body and mind by closing your eyes and taking a couple of deep breaths. In order to effectively cleanse the crystal, your own mind and energy should be relaxed and try to get rid of distracting or negative thoughts. Relax your body and don't slouch. Try to empty your mind, and just gently put your thoughts aside.

Step #3: Once you've already meditated, you can now take out your crystals/ gems and set them to the creek/ river.

Chapter Four: Other Cleansing Methods for Your Crystals

Step #4: Place the crystals/ gems into the current obviously in a location where your stones will not be carried away. The current or natural rhythm of the river will clean your pieces.

Step #5: As the flowing water is cleansing your crystals/ gems, you should visualize the negative energies and impurities of the stones being washed off by the water.

Step #6: Once you've already felt in you that the crystals and gems are being cleansed, you can now take them out of the water.

Step #7: Let it dry using a cloth, or out in the sun for a couple of minutes before placing it back into the pouch/ containers.

Ocean

If for some reason you live near the ocean or you have a chance to go near it, it's a great way to cleanse your crystals or gems as it a very powerful body of water since the light from the sun and the moon continuously energize it, not to mention the very high salt content which can

Chapter Four: Other Cleansing Methods for Your Crystals

ultimately wash your crystal's impurities. The waves in the ocean are continuously shifting which means that the energy is constantly in motion. It'll be a great way to purify your crystals and gems in this body of water because it also re – energizes them. When you do decide to wash them in the ocean, you'll need to place your stones inside a mesh bag to ensure that you won't lose them, and so that the waves can freely wash over them. In order for you to attune yourself with this method of cleansing process, follow the steps below:

Step #1: Place the crystals/ gems inside your mesh bag, ideally one with a sturdy handle attached to it so that you can easily hold it as it gets washed over by the ocean waves.

Step #2: Find a spot near the shore where you can't be disturbed and where the waves can also reach you.

Step #3: Once you've found a spot, sit by the shore, and hold the mesh bag in the water. Once you're already settled, you

Chapter Four: Other Cleansing Methods for Your Crystals

can now close your eyes, relax your mind and body and start meditating for a few minutes.

Step #4: Take a couple of deep breaths. In order to effectively cleanse the crystal, your own mind and energy should be relaxed and try to get rid of distracting or negative thoughts. Relax your body and don't slouch. Try to empty your mind, and just gently put your thoughts aside.

Step #5: As you meditate, feel the peaceful surrounding around you. Start visualizing the ocean's water cleansing your crystals and gems. Whenever the waves retreat back to the ocean, visualize your crystals negative energies being carried away with them. You can meditate for as long as necessary, or once you've felt that your stones have been completely cleansed.

Step #6: Once you're ready, open your eyes and pick up the mesh bag. Dry your crystals/ gems naturally or using a soft cloth before placing them back to their containers.

Chapter Four: Other Cleansing Methods for Your Crystals

Sunlight

The rays of the sun can be a great source of not just cleansing your stones but also re – energizing them. You can also cleanse some of your crystals by placing them under direct sunlight at your house like in the windowsill or in your backyard.

For this type of cleansing method, you just pretty much need your crystals/ gems that require cleansing. It's ideal to do this during sunrise or sunset. Do not set your stones out after sunrise or prior to sunset or during mid – day because the heat can damage your crystals/ gems. In order for you to attune yourself with this method of cleansing process, follow the steps below:

Step #1: Find a spot where your stones are safe under the direct sunlight.

Step #2: Place your crystals/ gems on your chosen spot. Sit down near it, as the rays of the sun shines upon your stones. You don't really need to sit next to your crystals under the

Chapter Four: Other Cleansing Methods for Your Crystals

sun so just find a spot near them where you won't be disturbed during your meditation.

Step #3: You can now start relaxing your body and mind by closing your eyes and taking a couple of deep breaths. In order to effectively cleanse the crystal, your own mind and energy should be relaxed and try to get rid of distracting or negative thoughts. Relax your body and don't slouch. Try to empty your mind, and just gently put your thoughts aside.

Step #4: Imagine the power of the rays of the sun removing all the negative energies and impurities from your crystals/ gemstones.

Step #5: Meditate for around 10 to 20 minutes or whenever you feel that your stones are thoroughly cleansed. Finish your meditation through imagining your crystals in your mind's eye totally clean from all unwanted energies. You can now use your purified crystals/ gems.

Chapter Four: Other Cleansing Methods for Your Crystals

Moonlight

Just like the rays of the sun, the light from the moon at night is another powerful way to cleanse your stones. For this type of cleansing method, you just pretty much need your crystals/ gems that require cleansing. You can do this at any phase of the moon but it's ideal if you do it during Full Moon and New Moon. As the moon wanes, any impurities and negative energies from your crystals will be effectively removed. In order for you to attune yourself with this method of cleansing process, follow the steps below:

Step #1: Find a spot where your stones are safe under the direct moon light.

Step #2: Place your crystals/ gems on your chosen spot. Sit down near it, as the moon light shines upon your stones. You don't really need to sit next to your crystals under the moon so just find a spot near them where you won't be disturbed during your meditation.

Step #3: You can now start relaxing your body and mind by closing your eyes and taking a couple of deep breaths. In

Chapter Four: Other Cleansing Methods for Your Crystals

order to effectively cleanse the crystal, your own mind and energy should be relaxed and try to get rid of distracting or negative thoughts. Relax your body and don't slouch. Try to empty your mind, and just gently put your thoughts aside.

Step #4: Imagine the power of the moon light removing all the negative energies and impurities from your crystals/ gemstones.

Step #5: Meditate for around 10 to 20 minutes or whenever you feel that your stones are thoroughly cleansed. Finish your meditation through imagining your crystals in your mind's eye totally clean from all unwanted energies. You can now use your purified crystals/ gems.

Earth or Soil

The earth is filled with various types of energy that can heal, comfort, cleanse, and balance. You can utilize the soil from your garden or even from your plant box to clean your crystals from its impurities. If possible, don't use a soil that's been sprayed with pesticide or has some type of fertilizer. Here are the things you need to prepare:

Chapter Four: Other Cleansing Methods for Your Crystals

Materials:

- A patch of soil from your garden or plant box (w/ or w/o plant)
- Hand shovel
- Crystals/ Gemstones

In order for you to attune yourself with this method of cleansing process, follow the steps below:

Step #1: Find a quiet spot in your garden or backyard where you can bury your crystals/ gems and where you won't be disturbed. You can then sit down comfortably near your stones and prepare yourself for meditation. If ever you chose to use a pot of soil, bring it with you and have your hand shovel/ crystals ready.

Step #2: You can now start relaxing your body and mind by closing your eyes and taking a couple of deep breaths. In order to effectively cleanse the crystal, your own mind and energy should be relaxed and try to get rid of distracting or

Chapter Four: Other Cleansing Methods for Your Crystals

negative thoughts. Relax your body and don't slouch. Try to empty your mind, and just gently put your thoughts aside.

Step #3: Once you've already relaxed and settled, you can open your eyes and pick up the shovel.

Step #4: Dig out a space where you can place your stone/s. Try not to dig too deeply especially if you're going to clean small gems so as not to lose your gemstones. Dig just deep enough to make your crystals and gems fully covered by the soil.

Step #5: Once you've done step #4, you can then place your crystals/ gems but make sure to create a space between them.

Step #6: Cover your stones completely with soil, and start meditating. Imagine that the natural powers of the earth are removing the unwanted energies and impurities. Meditate for as long as you feel is necessary.

Chapter Four: Other Cleansing Methods for Your Crystals

Step #7: You can leave the stones buried overnight but make sure to mark the spot where you buried them otherwise you might forget it in the morning. Dig them out as soon as you wake up, rinse them and let it dry.

Important Tip:

Since you are working with the Earth, it is best that you are not hungry if you choose to do this cleansing method. Make sure to have a light meal before you begin this activity.

It's also best to bury your gems/ crystals in a place where other people or animals can't access it. Find a spot where you can safely bury your stones and where only can access it.

Sea Salt

Sea salt has been used in different cleansing rituals throughout the centuries. It can be mixed with water to purify, heal and cleansed materials. It is primarily used to ward off any negative energy apart from using it as mixtures and solutions. Keep in mind that sea salt must be used when cleaning your stones, not table salt. This is because table salt

Chapter Four: Other Cleansing Methods for Your Crystals

has been processed already plus it may already contain chemicals. You can easily buy sea salt from your local stores. Here are the things you need to prepare:

Materials:

- A shallow glass container (this is where you will place crystals/ gems as well as the sea salt)
- Sea salt
- Crystals/ Gemstones

In order for you to attune yourself with this method of cleansing process, follow the steps below:

Step #1: Choose a place where you can do this cleansing activity without any disturbance. Bring all the materials with you, and sit down comfortably.

Step #2: You can now start relaxing your body and mind by closing your eyes and taking a couple of deep breaths. In order to effectively cleanse the crystal, your own mind and energy should be relaxed and try to get rid of distracting or

Chapter Four: Other Cleansing Methods for Your Crystals

negative thoughts. Relax your body and don't slouch. Try to empty your mind, and just gently put your thoughts aside.

Step #3: Once you've already relaxed, you can now start placing a layer of sea salt inside the glass container.

Step #4: Place your crystals and gemstones on the bed of salt

Step #5: Meditate for a couple of minutes, then imagine the natural cleansing powers of the sea salt removing any impurities from your crystals/ gems. Do this for as long as you feel is necessary.

Step #6: Let the crystals/ gems rest upon the bed of salt for a couple of hours to a few days or until you feel that is have been thoroughly cleansed. You will have an intuitive nudge once the stones are completely cleansed.

Step #7: When the crystals/ gems, you can then rinse it to remove the traces of salt. Dispose the sea salt after using it.

Chapter Four: Other Cleansing Methods for Your Crystals

Herbs and Dried Flowers

Certain dried flowers and herbs have also been known to purify and clean materials including crystals and gemstones. You can now use these herbs just like how you used sea salt to clean your stones. Here are a few herbs that you can use for this cleansing method:

- Acacia
- Basil
- Bay
- Carnation
- Cedar
- Eucalyptus
- Frankincense
- Hyssop
- Irish Moss
- Juniper
- Lavender
- Lemon Verbena
- Lemongrass
- Mugwort
- Myrrh
- Peppermint
- Red Clover
- Rose Petals
- Rosemary
- Sage
- Sandalwood
- St. John's Wort
- Star Anise
- Sweetgrass
- Thyme
- Valerian Root
- Vervain
- Witch Hazel
- Yarrow

Chapter Four: Other Cleansing Methods for Your Crystals

Select the herbs that you want to cleanse your crystals and gems. You can choose one herb or with a combination of dried flowers if you like. Here are the things you need to prepare:

Materials:

- A shallow glass container (this is where you will place crystals/ gems as well as the dried flowers/ herbs)
- Herbs/ Dried Flowers
- Crystals/ Gemstones

In order for you to attune yourself with this method of cleansing process, follow the steps below:

Step #1: Choose a place where you can do this cleansing activity without any disturbance. Bring all the materials with you, and sit down comfortably.

Step #2: You can now start relaxing your body and mind by closing your eyes and taking a couple of deep breaths. In

Chapter Four: Other Cleansing Methods for Your Crystals

order to effectively cleanse the crystal, your own mind and energy should be relaxed and try to get rid of distracting or negative thoughts. Relax your body and don't slouch. Try to empty your mind, and just gently put your thoughts aside.

Step #3: Once you've already relaxed, you can now start placing a bed of herbs inside the glass container. You can also trim any long pieces so that you can easily mix the herbs.

Step #4: Place your crystals and gemstones on the bed of herbs/ dried flowers.

Step #5: Meditate for a couple of minutes, then imagine the natural cleansing powers of the herbs/ dried flowers removing any impurities from your crystals/ gems. Do this for as long as you feel is necessary.

Step #6: Let the crystals/ gems rest upon the bed of herbs for a couple of hours to a few days or until you feel that is have

Chapter Four: Other Cleansing Methods for Your Crystals

been thoroughly cleansed. You will have an intuitive nudge once the stones are completely cleansed.

Step #7: When the crystals/ gems, you can then rinse it to remove the traces of herbs. Dispose the herbs/ dried flowers after using it.

Quartz Crystals

Quartz crystals can be used to cleanse impurities from crystals and gems though you will need to have a large collection of these because a single quartz will not be effective. In order for you to attune yourself with this method of cleansing process, follow the steps below:

Step #1: Make sure that your collection of quartz crystals has been cleansed to make it an effective tool to clean your other crystals/ gems.

Step #2: You can now start relaxing your body and mind by closing your eyes and taking a couple of deep breaths. In order to effectively cleanse the crystal, your own mind and energy should be relaxed and try to get rid of distracting or

Chapter Four: Other Cleansing Methods for Your Crystals

negative thoughts. Relax your body and don't slouch. Try to empty your mind, and just gently put your thoughts aside.

Step #3: Open your eyes after meditating for a couple of minutes; you can now place your crystals/ gems on top or beside the cluster of quartz crystals as long as it is not touching the cluster itself.

Step #4: Meditate for a couple of minutes, then imagine the natural cleansing powers of the cluster of quartz removing any impurities from your crystals/ gems. Do this for as long as you feel is necessary.

Step #5: Leave your stones in contact with the cluster of quartz crystals until you feel an intuitive nudge that they are already completely cleansed. This can take a day or so.

Step #6: Once the cleansing process is done, you can now use your stones. Remember to also clean your cluster of quartz crystals after using it.

Chapter Four: Other Cleansing Methods for Your Crystals

Tips When Cleansing Your Gemstones and Crystals

In addition to knowing how to properly cleanse your stones, you should keep in mind some tips for the cleansing activity as effective as possible:

Tip #1: Never allow your stones to be handled by other people

The reason why you have to clean your crystals prior to using them is to remove any unwanted traces of energy that the stone has absorbed from people who touched the stone before you bought it. Your crystal prior to cleansing have absorbed energies from people or objects where it was once stored. Once you have thoroughly cleansed your crystals/ gems, don't let other people handle or play with them so as not to sort of contaminate it with other energies.

Tip #2: Cleanse your stones as often as necessary.

Cleansing your stones should be done every time you use your crystals/ gems, or as soon as you acquire them. Repeat the process as often as needed. It's ideal to cleanse your stones prior and after using them especially if you have used it to absorb negative impurities, or heal someone with

Chapter Four: Other Cleansing Methods for Your Crystals

an illness. Never store your stones with your other collection if you haven't cleansed it yet so as not to contaminate the rest of your crystals.

Tip #3: A thoroughly cleansed crystal/ gem are in its most effective state.

If your stones are untouched for quite a long period of time, they may lose their energy and can therefore become less effective. You will still need to clean your crystal in order to remove any stale energy due to storage.

Tip #4: Do not clean you crystals/ gems when you're in a hurry.

As what you've read in the last sections, you need to prepare the materials and meditate first before you do the cleansing process which means that you need to make sure you have plenty of time, and not shortcut the process. It's also ideal to be physically clean before you do the cleansing process because it will help your body to also relax and feel pure. Give your undivided attention whenever you're doing this activity so that your crystals/ gems will also feel

Chapter Four: Other Cleansing Methods for Your Crystals

recharged and renewed. You also need to make sure that each of your crystals receives sufficient time and care.

Caring Tips for Your Gemstones and Crystals

Aside from cleansing your crystals and gemstones from all types of impurities, proper care and handling is also essential to the effectiveness of your stones. Below are some tips on how you can ensure that your crystals/ gems are handled and kept in a way that will maximize their natural energy.

Tip #1: Never leave your crystals/ gems on rough surfaces
Your crystals/ gems may get minor damages and scratches that can affect its performance and its luster.

Tip #2: Never leave your crystals/ gems out in the open (sun / rain) for an extended period of time.
As mentioned earlier, you shouldn't leave your crystals throughout the day especially under the scorching heat of the sun; you should follow a certain time period. This

Chapter Four: Other Cleansing Methods for Your Crystals

is the same if you're going to cleanse the stones in the rain, you should pick it up after the shower and don't leave it for a long time. Keep in mind that your crystals require both physical and psychic level of attunement.

Tip #3: If you're going to travel with your crystals/ gems, make sure to wrap them separately using a cotton or silk fabric.

Each of the crystal should be wrapped separately because they contain different energies. Never place heavy objects on top of the crystals even if they're wrapped up. You can also use pure wool if you like.

Tip #4: Don't store your crystals/ gems in a place or location where their energies can be sucked out.

Placing these crystals near gadgets or objects with electromagnetic fields like laptops, computers, cellphones, or TV can disrupt the natural energy flow of your stones. Try not to store them near electronic devices. Even if some crystals are meant to suck the electromagnetic energy off of

Chapter Four: Other Cleansing Methods for Your Crystals

your devices, you will need to keep them in a neutral place or cleanse them every day.

It's very important to know how to cleanse and care for your stones as much as you know how to use them because if you don't, it will definitely affect their performance as well as their connection with you. You see, these stones are not just powerful and aesthetically pleasing, they are very much alive, just like the plants you have outside because they also contain energy and the so – called consciousness of the Universe. It's important to use them properly and treat them with respect just like how a martial artist treats their weapons. What these stones can do for you is only limited by your knowledge and imagination.

Chapter Five: Crystals and Their Benefits

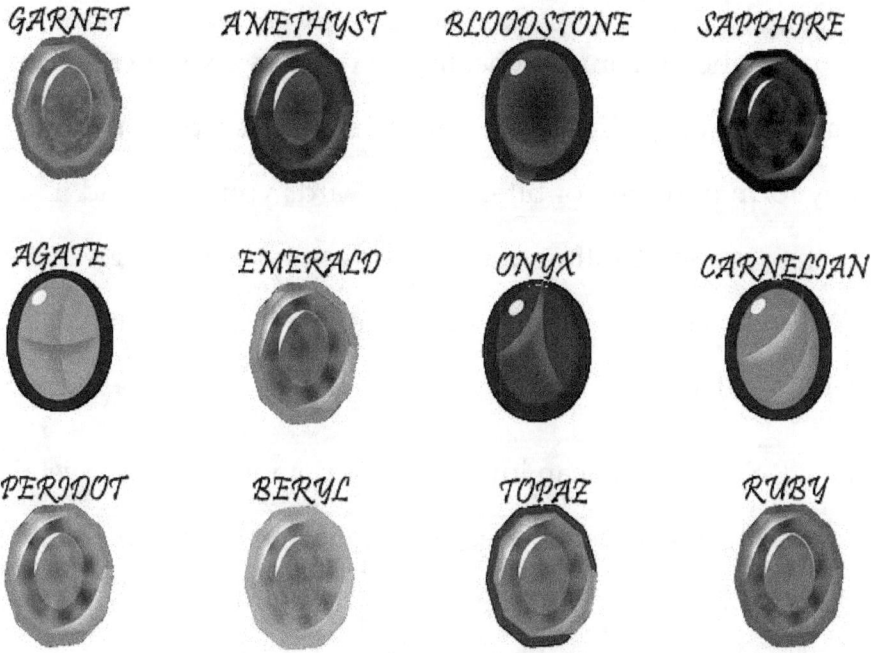

Crystals and their Uses

Agate

for healing, protection, physical/ emotional balance, and grounding.

How it can help you:

This crystal can help you become grounded as it creates a physical and emotional balance. It will help an individual get in touch with both their physical and emotional state and create balance within one's soul.

When it comes to healing, it can be very effective for emotional level of healing. This crystal frees a person from any form of hatred or bitterness towards your foes and it helps a person to show compassion and practice forgiveness. Agate is a crystal than can help a person in a peacefully emotional state.

Since Agate can influence your emotions, this crystal can also protect you from physical and mental drain. It can prevent dark and depressing thoughts as well as bad dreams. It helps a person to quickly release feelings of sadness, negativity, and anger.

Alexandrite
for self – confidence and good luck.

How it can help you:

This crystal is known to bring good fortune. It can help a person to attract joyful and loving energies. And if one is surrounded with positive energies, an individual tend to become a 'magnet' of good luck. Alexandrite also banishes any negative thoughts, and it inspires a person to see one's strengths instead of insecurities. When you have self – respect, you'll be drawn to people who are the same, and they will also respect you.

Amber

for happiness and healing.

How it can help you:

Amber is used for helping a sick person towards a speedy recovery because it can absorb negative energies caused by an illness/ ailments. It also takes away emotional and mental burden as well as the feelings of helplessness. Once Amber absorbed such negative energies, you may see that the quality of the stone becomes cloudier than before which is why after every use, you should cleanse it as soon as possible.

This stone can transform negative energies into positive ones making you filled with positive vibes. Once you are free from any mentally and emotionally burdensome feelings/ thoughts, you will then allow healing and happiness to come to you which can help you recover faster. Any negative energy flowing unto you is removed by

Chapter Five: Crystals and their Benefits

this crystal which is why you may experience a feeling of lightness after working with it.

In addition to removing such negative vibes, it can also help a person maintain its positive mental state. When you're in a positive state, healing is much quicker whereas if you're always feeling down, it will also tend to slow down your recovery. Amber also unlocks one's healing energies

Amethyst

for Sleep, focus, healing, concentration.

How it can help you:

Amethyst is a very powerful healing crystal, and it can be used to heal ailments whether it is on a physical, emotional, mental or spiritual level. Amethyst is a vital element that can aid and fasten healing. It can help soothe one's mind and calms any stressful thoughts as well as negative vibes that can affect the physical state. Amethyst can bring out the natural healing powers of a person, and it will flow more freely especially if an individual is in a positive state.

Chapter Five: Crystals and their Benefits

In addition to its healing powers, amethyst can help a person be focused on tasks that needs concentration. It can be used during meditation, and can aid when a magician is performing healing rituals to an ill person.

Amethyst can help direct and strengthened one's ability to focus, making a person become more efficient and effective on the task at hand. Try using it when you need to focus on memorizing something, writing, presenting, planning or studying. A clear mind can accomplish task with speed and accuracy, and it can also reach a deeper state during meditation.

Angelite
for communication.

How it can help you:

This crystal aids in expression or communication. It helps an individual express something and also opens one to receive/ understand the message of other people. It enhances one's ability to reach to someone even if they are physically far. It also help heightens awareness on a psychic level

Chapter Five: Crystals and their Benefits

which can allow a person to become more receptive to communicating from other beings in a higher level/ realm.

A person's ability to understand other people on a much deeper level is aided by Angelite. In most cases, our understanding of other people is only on the surface or from a logical/ rational perspective. This stone helps one to connect with others on a more spiritual level. It will help you communicate with them, and express yourself freely and clearly. Angelite can help a person articulate something that's hard to say, or something that may require courage – like telling the truth.

Emerald

for love, healing, focus, harmony, quick thinking

How it can help you:

The stone of emerald can be very powerful in helping a person to calm one's mind. It allows one to focus and concentrate more clearly. Having a piece of emerald on your work desk or carrying it with you around especially during meetings and important events that requires concentration can be very effective in helping one to stay focused.

Emerald is also used as a healing stone whether it is on a physical, emotional, mental or spiritual level. This stone can help remove any stressful/ negative thoughts making a person recover quickly from physical illness. When dealing with emotional pain or heart aches, emerald can be held close to the heart particularly during meditation as it emits a comforting and soothing vibe. It can also help in creating a loving and harmonious atmosphere which is why it's an ideal stone to be place at home particularly in places where people gather.

Fluorite

for healing and balance

How it can help you:

Flourite heals by removing any negative energy that could be affecting your physical, emotional, and mental state. As it banishes negative vibes, it can make a person more susceptible to positive energy. It also helps in re – energizing one's body and mind. Flourite, also known as the "mind stone," can also increase intelligence and it creates a balance between one's emotional and mental self. It makes

Chapter Five: Crystals and their Benefits

one see a situation from a balanced perspective since it clears one's head. It will help you in considering problems, provides resolutions, and help during decision – making instances.

Hematite

for harmony in relationships, and grounding

How it can help you:

Hematite is a crystal that is best for grounding oneself. It helps gather scattered energies, allows a person to concentrate, and be in a calm state. Hematite removes any negative energy which is why it's ideal to place it inside a house or a room that may always be filled with tension or conflict. It helps restore harmony and balance as well as improves relationships.

Chapter Five: Crystals and their Benefits

Howlite

for calming, reasoning, and soothing

How it can help you:

This is a stone that can enhance a person's rational or reasoning abilities. It makes an individual more patient, calm, and to look at things from a rational perspective. It can help one to communicate effectively with others because it emits soothing and calming energies, and also aids in finding resolutions quickly. You can carry it in your pocket especially if you are feeling angry or anxious at the moment so that you won't take out your frustrations on other people. It also prevents you from absorbing other people's anger or anxiety.

Jade

for protection, wealth, harmony, love, relaxation

How it can help you:

The stone of Jade can aid in creating a harmonious atmosphere as well as reduce tensions and provides soothing and calming energies. It can also be used for protection as it can shield a person from negative energies being thrown by other people.

Jade is also a great stone to wear as jewelry or carry in one's pocket especially if you're trying to find love. It can also be powerful to attract money and wealth as it opens your mind to financial or wealth opportunities. You can choose to place a Jade stone in your house or business place so that wealth can be drawn to you. It also helps in clearing one's mind when it comes to making financial decisions and important negotiations as it energy influences a person to determine the best course of action to increase one's wealth.

Quartz Crystal

for meditation, healing, inner peace, harmony, balancing, cleansing

How it can help you:

These stones are rich with natural psychic energies making it a very powerful crystal. It's very effective even if you use just a piece of it. It can turn negative energies into positive ones and can also ward off any impurities, which is why it's also a cleansing tool for other crystals and gemstones. Quartz crystals are very helpful during meditation because it helps a person to focus and increase one's psychic level. It enables an individual to reach a much deeper state of consciousness.

It's also known for being a balancing stone because it gathers scattered energies, removes blockage, and promotes energy flow within an individual. It cleanses and heals a person and it also aligns one's chakras. You or your house can be in perfect harmony if this stone is around.

Rose Quartz

for self – confidence, attracting love, balanced emotions, beauty, self - love

How it can help you:

This quartz is also known as the "love stone." It is filled with all kinds of love energy; love for oneself, for other people, and for romantic love. Magicians advise people to carry this stone in order to enhance acceptance and self – love as well as to appreciate beauty, skills, talent etc. Rose Quartz can help the energy of love to grow within you and radiates from you which can attract similar emotions from other people. It also tends to magnify one's physical and inner beauty that can cause others to feel a sense of grace by your mere presence. It also balances energy so that an individual will not be overwhelmed by so much good emotions.

Ruby

for Love

How it can help you:

Another stone that can attract romantic love as well as self – love is Ruby. It aids in creating a healthy balance of self – love and love of others. It also helps in alleviating the fear of being in a relationship if ever an individual had been heartbroken before. It also helps rekindle passionate feelings of love between couples.

Sapphire

for happiness, inner peace, clarity, love, wish fulfillment

How it can help you:

The stone of Sapphire align and balances one's thoughts so that a person experiencing it would not be overwhelmed. It helps a person to have a clear mind which can be useful if one is making a decision especially when stakes are high. It clears one's mind and creates inner peace.

Sapphire can also uplift one's spirit, and allows a person to feel the joy and love surrounding him/her. It also helps in keeping an open eye to the many blessings and grace that many people may fail to see because of negative thinking.

It can also become a personal wishing stone as it complements positive energies which mean that it can help fulfill your desires and wishes. You can work with the energies contain in Sapphire especially when you want to manifest something into your life.

Chapter Five: Crystals and their Benefits

Tourmaline

for positive thinking, inspiration, balance

How it can help you:

Tourmaline is also known as the "inspiration stone" simply because it stimulates one's creativity. Using this stone can create a good flow of energy, and also bring forth inner passion. A person can use this to encourage the mind of creating ideas and attracting positive energy. You will begin to have a sense of accomplishment, feel lighter, and it also helps in balancing energies flowing through you.

Tourmaline can also aid in maintaining the right level of energy that will help a person in utilizing one's abilities without physically, emotionally, and mentally draining the body.

Turquoise

for protection, strengthening friendships, forming friendships, communication, warding off negative vibes, healing

Chapter Five: Crystals and their Benefits

How it can help you:

Turquoise is another powerful healing stone as it helps in speedy recovery regardless if the illness is physical or emotional. It wards off any negative energy that aggravates conditions and it also protects a person from harmful energies. This stone magnifies the body's ability to naturally heal and restore thereby speeding up the healing process. It's a remarkable healing stone that magicians use when performing healing rituals.

Turquoise can also help a person in becoming a good communicator, and it enhances one's ability to connect with other people and with spiritual beings. It makes an individual become more receptive to information as well. It's ideal to carry this stone wherever or wear it as a jewelry if you want to easily get along with other people especially those who you do not know yet. It can help build new relationships/ friendships as well as strengthen or rekindle existing friendships.

Chapter Five: Crystals and their Benefits

Aquamarine

for calm, and intuition

How it can help you:

The stone of Aquamarine is usually linked with the ocean making its powers related to that of water. Since water has a calming and relaxing effect, aquamarine also provides the same effect to a person. Water is also linked with a person's subconscious which is why this stone can help one to become attune with one's intuition or inner voice.

It's also a great crystal to use during meditation due to its peaceful energy, and it can be used whenever you are feeling agitation or recurring thoughts due to certain circumstances. It soothes and calms a person and it makes an individual become more comfortable with oneself. It can also help you become more patient and understanding to other people. This stone can calm one's mind and allows a person to hear one's inner self. It's very important that you know how to listen and follow your intuition; the stone of aquamarine can free you from other negative voices or thoughts and worries.

Chapter Five: Crystals and their Benefits

Aventurine

for leadership, prosperity, healing, money and financial luck

How it can help you:

The stone of Aventurine heals and strengthens the body's natural healing process. It also removes anxiety and stress. Aside from its healing energies, it can also increase one's leadership skills and self – confidence as well as promote a strong spirit/ personality.

Aventurine can be a helpful when it comes to attracting wealth and financial matters. If you carry this stone or wear it as jewelry, it can make you a money magnet. It can also influence your psyche and draw financial opportunities towards you.

Citrine

for wealth, motivation, clarity, intuition, warding off negative energy, positive thinking

How it can help you:

This stone can help an individual to have a clarity of mind and helps a person attune to one's inner voice. It removes any negative thoughts and maintains positive vibes. The citrine stone can also be very powerful when it comes to drawing abundance and wealth into one's life. Placing a Citrine stone in the area where you conduct business can attract wealth and prosperity. It also helps an individual to manage their finances. It's highly recommended to put a piece of citrine in your wallet as it can help draw more money. Citrine's positive energy can also inspire a person and make one become more creative and motivated especially when working on an important project.

Garnet

for success, protection, emotional comfort, good health

How it can help you:

The stone of Garnet has good energies that can help a person maintain good health. It also protects an individual from harmful energies and creates a balance to the flow of energy coming in and out of the body. You can also use Garnet to let go of any negative feelings as it can help in providing warm and soothing vibes that can comfort you during times of anxiety and stress. When trying to let go of a relationship or going through a tough one, this stone can create emotional balance enabling one to feel calmer amidst feelings of frustration, anger, or regret.

When it comes to any endeavors, or success in business, this stone can magnify one's efforts and increase positive energies that could bring forth success to an individual.

Herkimer Diamond

for uplifting one's spirit, enhanced energy, dream recall

How it can help you:

Herkimer Diamond has a double – terminated characteristic that can enhance a powerful energy which can be very useful in manifesting a specific intention. It's a very powerful and flexible type of Quartz Crystal than can enhance energy in almost any situation.

Herkimer Diamond can be a very powerful stone to help a person remember one's dreams. It can be of great use whenever you're trying to interpret your dreams or even when connecting with higher spiritual beings. You can also use this stone to uplift your spirit especially when you're feeling uninspired, depressed or filled with worries. Its powerful and positive energies can make you be in a better mood.

Chapter Six: Methods and Instructions for Using Crystals

Methods for Attracting Love

The methods that will be mentioned in this section can help you to invite love into your life. It doesn't only pertain to romantic love or love between couples/ spouses but it's also oriented towards love for other people like friends and family. After practicing a certain method, it's plausible that you might meet someone special which could

Chapter Six: Methods and Instructions for Using Crystals

lead you to finding your true love, or you can end up attracting your soul mate.

Such methods can also aid you in creating a much deeper relationship with other people, increase your "love tank," be more caring towards others, and also get to enjoy your existing and future relationships. In any case, the methods given here can yield positive results and expand the love energy that already surrounds you that can draw the right people in your life. Whenever you do apply the techniques here, it's ideal to not think of any specific person because this could block you to the possibility of finding the love you deserve since you are only locking your attention to one outcome. It's prudent to keep your mind and heart open, and learn to TRUST the powers of the Universe.

Attracting Someone Who Shares Your Interests

Do this method if you want to attract someone who has pretty much the same interests that you have. It's not necessarily limited to a romantic lover as you can also end up finding a true friend or colleague which can turn your life around – though the purpose of this technique is to invite

Chapter Six: Methods and Instructions for Using Crystals

someone whom you can share your joy and interests with the possibility of falling in love.

Prepare the following items:

- Pink or rose – colored candle
- Vanilla Oil
- Fireproof dish
- Match or lighter
- Bowl of sunflower seeds
- Ring (containing any of these gems; Emerald, Ruby, Jade, Rose Quartz, Pink Tourmaline, Sapphire)

Instructions:

Step #1: Find a quiet spot where you won't be disturbed.

Step #2: Bring all the materials you need with you. Sit down and meditate by closing your eyes, taking deep breaths, and relaxing your body. Try to be at peace and empty your mind.

Step #3: Open your eyes whenever you're ready to start.

Chapter Six: Methods and Instructions for Using Crystals

Step #4: Pour vanilla oil unto the pink candle. You can rub the oil on the sides of the candle until it's completely anointed with it. While doing this, try to imagine a person who shares your interests being drawn to you, in a way that he/she is attracted to the scent of the vanilla oil.

Step #5: Place the pink candle on the fireproof dish and light it up. Spend some time gazing at the candle flame. As the candle burns, know that the person with whom you share your joy with will be guided towards you through the light.

Step #6: Using the candle's light, you can then energize the sunflower seeds. Create a small layer of the seeds within the bowl and make sure to evenly spread it out. This is how your ring will be energized. Close your eyes while your hands are placed over the bowl of seeds. Imagine a pink – colored light emanating from your hands to the sunflower seeds; visualize yourself charging the seeds with energies of love.

Step #7: Once you felt that the seeds are filled with enough amounts of love energies, you can now open your eyes and

Chapter Six: Methods and Instructions for Using Crystals

place your ring on it. This will allow the powerful love energies of the ring to combine with yours.

Step #8: Leave the ring on the bed of seeds until the candle is burned down so that it can fully absorb and combine with your love energy.

Step #9: Once the candle has burned down, you can now take the ring and wear it. Keep an open heart and mind to attract the right person and in order for that person to find his/her way to you.

How to Draw the Right Lover

This method will make you physically and inwardly attractive to the right person for you. The crystals and gems for this technique will help in magnifying not just your beauty but also your best qualities. You will then send out energies that can lead you to the right lover.

Prepare the following items:

- 8 pieces of red or pink rose petals

Chapter Six: Methods and Instructions for Using Crystals

- Small drawstring pouch
- Any of these crystals: Ruby, Rose Quartz, and Pink Tourmaline

Instructions:

Step #1: Find a quiet spot where you won't be disturbed.

Step #2: Bring all the materials you need with you. Sit down and meditate by closing your eyes, taking deep breaths, and relaxing your body. Try to be at peace and empty your mind.

Step #3: Open your eyes whenever you're ready to start.

Step #4: Get your drawstring pouch and place the petals and stone inside before closing it.

Step #5: Clasp the pouch using both of your hands and put it near your heart. Close your eyes then take deep breaths and feel the beating of your heart against the pouch. What you're doing here is filling the pouch with your love energy. Allow yourself to feel loved, secured, and happy. Pour these emotions into the pouch you're holding.

Chapter Six: Methods and Instructions for Using Crystals

Step #6: Once you're done, you can now open your eyes and know that it's already filled with love energies which will draw the right lover for you. Carry this pouch wherever you go, and you can also place it under your pillow. Do this technique or carry it with you until the right one comes along.

How to Invite Love in Your Life by Preparing Yourself Mentally, Emotionally and Physically

Another simple method of attracting love in your life is through preparing a love inviting bath. Through placing the stone in a bathwater, you can be mentally, emotionally and physically cleansed which can make you more charming and attractive to other people.

Prepare any of the following items:

- Rose Quartz (best)
- Pink Tourmaline
- Emerald (make sure the water is not too hot)
- Ruby

Chapter Six: Methods and Instructions for Using Crystals

- Jade

Instructions:

Step #1: Run your bath. You can use various products like shower gel, bath salts, scented candles or anything that makes you feel refreshed and energized.

Step #2: Place the crystals in your bath water and imagine its energies being released and giving power to the water.

Step #3: Get into your bath tub and hold the crystal. Close your eyes and relax. Imagine the love energy covering your entire being and flowing through you. You can do this for as long as you want.

Step #4: Once you felt that you have already absorbed all the love energies, you can now get out of your bath tub and take the crystal with you.

Step #5: As you dry yourself, know that the love energy is radiating in your entire being which will attract more feelings of love to you.

Chapter Six: Methods and Instructions for Using Crystals

Attracting New Friendships into Your Life

Wherever you go, you can make new friends by meeting people though sometimes it's not easy and oftentimes the connection is just shallow. Using the method and crystals below will help you in attracting new friends and send out an energy that makes people be drawn towards you.

Prepare the following items:

- Pink or rose – colored candle
- Fireproof dish
- Match or lighter
- Any of these gems; Emerald, Ruby, Turquoise, Rose Quartz, Dendritic Agate, Pink Tourmaline, Sapphire)

Instructions:

Step #1: Find a quiet spot where you won't be disturbed.

Step #2: Bring all the materials you need with you. Sit down and meditate by closing your eyes, taking deep breaths, and relaxing your body. Try to be at peace and empty your mind.

Chapter Six: Methods and Instructions for Using Crystals

Step #3: Open your eyes whenever you're ready to start.

Step #4: The candle should be placed on a holder or a fireproof dish. Light it up and know that as you do this, you are inviting new friendships and people to come into your life.

Step #5: Take the crystal in your hands and close your eyes. Imagine new friends coming into your life, and that you have a strong and healthy relationship with them. Feel the happiness and the warmth of their love, and as you start feeling these wonderful emotions, channel it to the stone and charge it with these love energy.

Step #6: Once you're done, open your eyes and give a gentle kiss to the stone. Then, place the candle on a safe spot with your crystal lying beside it. Make sure to light it every day until the candle completely burns down.

Step #7: Once the candle has completely burned down, you can now carry the crystal with you wherever you go and do so until you have formed all the friendships that you like. It will also help you sustain these new friendships and form a much deeper connection with them.

Chapter Six: Methods and Instructions for Using Crystals

Methods for Attracting Prosperity and Wealth

The methods in this section are intended to attract prosperity and abundance into your life. It's not only about attracting money or anything related to success in business but also in various forms like friendship, health, and simple joys. Use the methods below to draw any forms of abundance in your life.

Attracting Money and Success

This method can aid you if you want to ensure success of a particular business endeavor. There are times where conflicts arise because people involved may not be focused on the same goals. The technique below will help you with such business – related projects:

Prepare the following items:

- Green or orange candle
- Fireproof dish
- Match or lighter
- Cinnamon Oil

Chapter Six: Methods and Instructions for Using Crystals

- Any or combination of these crystals/ gems: Citrine (for motivation between team members), Rose Quartz (for creating balance among team members), and Aventurine (for attracting abundance and success energies).

Instructions:

Step #1: Find a quiet spot where you won't be disturbed.

Step #2: Bring all the materials you need with you. Sit down and meditate by closing your eyes, taking deep breaths, and relaxing your body. Try to be at peace and empty your mind.

Step #3: Open your eyes whenever you're ready to start.

Step #4: Anoint the orange or green candle with cinnamon oil.

Step #5: Pour cinnamon oil unto the candle. You can rub the oil on the sides of the candle until it's completely anointed with it. While doing this, try to imagine a certain business or project that you want to be successful. Visualize that you are lighting the "torch" of your success.

Chapter Six: Methods and Instructions for Using Crystals

Step #6: Place the candle on the fireproof dish and light it up. Spend some time gazing at the candle flame. As the candle burns, feel and imagine the feelings of success and how it's burning up within you.

Step #7: Place the stone around the fireproof dish or candle holder one at a time. For instance, as you put down the Citrine crystal, imagine you and your team members becoming motivated and inspired to finish the task at hand. If you use Rose Quartz, imagine the team harmoniously working with one another and complementing each other's roles in the project. If you use Aventurine, imagine the project being completed with great success.

Step #8: Now that the stone/s is in place, you can now close your eyes and imagine each of them forming a link with one another with such blazing energy. Imagine the individual powers of your stones combining and being guided by the light or torch of success. Know that the success and abundance energies are charging up your business endeavors.

Chapter Six: Methods and Instructions for Using Crystals

Step #9: Leave the stones beside the candle as it burns down. Once it's completely burned down, carry the crystals with you or place them in your working area.

Creating a Financial Lucky Charm

The method below will teach you on how you can create a magical pouch that will serve as your lucky charm when it comes to finances.

Prepare the following items:

- Gold – colored or yellow drawstring pouch
- Any of these gems/ crystals: Moss Agate, Dendritic Agate, Alexandrite, Jade
- A small amount of herbs (choose any of the following or combine them):
    - Cinnamon
    - Bay Leaves
    - Basil

Chapter Six: Methods and Instructions for Using Crystals

Instructions:

Step #1: Find a quiet spot where you won't be disturbed.

Step #2: Bring all the materials you need with you. Sit down and meditate by closing your eyes, taking deep breaths, and relaxing your body. Try to be at peace and empty your mind.

Step #3: Open your eyes whenever you're ready. Take the pouch and place the herbs inside it. Know that as you do this, the herbs have powerful energies that can attract abundance and prosperity. Visualize these prosperity energies being drawn towards you.

Step #4: Place the stones inside the pouch with the herbs. Close it and hold the pouch close to you using both of your hands. Close your eyes and imagine the herbs and the crystal working together to bring abundance and wealth into your life. Visualize the pouch drawing financial energies to you, and feel as if you're already rich and that you already possess the money or wealth that you desire.

Step #5: Once you're done, you can now open your eyes. Make sure to carry the pouch with you especially if you're going to financial/ business – related transactions, sales pitches, job interviews, performance appraisals, negotiations, salary increase requests etc.

How to Ensure That You Always Have the Money You Need

This is another simple technique that could be very effective for your personal finances. It's ideal that you make this method a regular part of your daily meditative routine so that your wallet will never run dry. Know that you already have the money that you need, and already feel the feelings of financial abundance even if you haven't manifested it yet. You can be almost certain that the Universe will provide you with whatever amount you need and you'll never experience lack in your financial life as long as you keep your mind and heart open for financial abundance and opportunities that are already surrounding you.

Chapter Six: Methods and Instructions for Using Crystals

Prepare the following items:

- Wallet/ Purse
- Bayberry oil
- Any of these gems:
- Jade
- Green Jade
- Emerald
- Sapphire
- Moss Agate
- Dendritic Agate
- Aventurine
- Ruby
- Green Tourmaline
- Citrine

Instructions:

Step #1: Anoint the crystal you chose to work with by pouring bayberry oil. You can also do the same with your coins and paper bills as well as your purse/ wallet. This is because it is believed that bayberry oil draws wealth and

Chapter Six: Methods and Instructions for Using Crystals

abundance energies. It's also best to anoint your money, wallet, and stone on a Thursday.

Step #2: Once you've finished the anointing ritual, you can now keep the stone inside your wallet. Obviously if it's not small enough to fit your wallet or purse, you can just carry it around in a pouch.

Step #3: Every Thursday, make it a habit to recharge the stone as well as your money and wallet so that it can continuously attract prosperity and wealth energies. As you do this practice, you'll become more confident and secured in handling your personal finances, and attract more of it. You'll soon notice that your wallet never runs dry.

Chapter Seven: Other Purposes of Crystals

Crystals for Emotional Balance

Worrisome thoughts and stressful experiences can cause a person to be emotionally imbalanced. If a person is emotionally stressed, it attracts depressing energies and causes a person to be angry, sad, regretful or agitated. The methods below will help you create a balance emotion within so that even if negative energies come to you, your mind and heart will not succumb to these feelings. These methods will also help you be more at peace and soothes your inner being during times of distress.

Chapter Seven: Other Purposes of Crystals

Crystals to Lift Your Spirit

There are times when experiences outside of our control get to us, and we feel the weight of the world in our shoulders. Such feelings of despair could be from a heartbreak, from sad moments, or anything that causes you to feel uninspired or depress. In any case, your stones can help uplift your weary spirit and also get rid of these negative emotions. Follow the instructions below and you'll eventually see how your crystals can work wonders for you.

Prepare the following items:

- Tea light or small candle
- Match or lighter
- Candle holder or fireproof dish
- Any of these gems:
  - Green Jade
  - Tourmaline
  - Moss Agate
  - Quartz Crystal
  - Flourite
  - Agate

Chapter Seven: Other Purposes of Crystals

- o Crazy Lace Agate
- o Green Flourite
- o Rose Quartz

Instructions:

Step #1: Find a quiet spot where you won't be disturbed. If you're doing the ritual during the day, make sure to close the windows/ curtains to prevent too much light on the inside. On the other hand, if you're doing it during the night, make sure that you put on dim lights.

Step #2: Bring all the materials you need with you. Sit down and meditate by closing your eyes, taking deep breaths, and relaxing your body. Try to be at peace and empty your mind.

Step #3: Open your eyes whenever you're ready to start. Place the candle on the holder or fireproof dish. Light it up and place the stone you chose near the candle in a way that its flame is reflected upon the crystal's surface.

Step #4: Become attuned with your crystal by visualizing an energetic vibration between you and your gem. Realize that

Chapter Seven: Other Purposes of Crystals

the vibrational link has always been there with the crystal when you acquired it. Communicate with your crystal and ask it to allow the negative emotions and feelings to dissipate as the candle melts away.

Step #5: Let your eyes rest on the reflection of the flame on the surface of your crystal. The reflection will look like your crystal's pulsating energy as the flame flickers. Realize that your crystal is at work in removing negative energies and dark thoughts off of you. And that your gem is replacing these negative vibes with happy and inspirational energies. Your crystal's power and your energies will together lift the veil of sad feelings away from you as the candle melts away.

Step #6: Continue concentrating on the reflection of the flame upon your crystal and keep your body and breathings relaxed. Try to empty your mind and free it of any distractions. Open your chest as you inhale and exhale, and eventually you'll feel that your heart is becoming less and less heavy. You start to feel lighter as the heavy burdens of sadness and negativity dissipates from you.

Step #7: Once the candle has completely burned down, realize that your sad and negative feelings are gone and was

Chapter Seven: Other Purposes of Crystals

released as the candle burns. After doing this, you can now pick up your gem and hold it in your heart. Thank your crystal for helping you uplift your being.

How to Ease Away from Emotional Distress

The method below will teach you how your stones can relieve you off your emotional pains/ distress. Sad or stressful thoughts go in and out of our mind throughout the day, and sometimes we're so busy that we don't seem to notice it. However, when you finally had the chance to relax and close your eyes, the negative thoughts that you've been ignoring all day is bombarding your mind that keeps you from having a good night sleep, then you carry these compounded thoughts the next day. The technique below will teach you how using your stones can help you distance yourself from all these negative energies, allowing you to have a restful sleep.

Prepare any of the following items:

- Garnet

Chapter Seven: Other Purposes of Crystals

- Pink Tourmaline
- Sapphire
- Purple Jade
- Moss Agate
- Crazy Lace Agate
- Agate

Instructions:

Step #1: Before you go to bed from a long day, take any of the crystals mentioned above on your bed side. It's best to place it under your pillow so that your head can feel the powerful energies of your stone as you lay upon it.

Step #2: Close your eyes and try to prevent falling asleep. Focus on your breathings and empty your mind. Try to relax your entire body and prepare yourself for a short meditation.

Step #3: Imagine your crystal beginning to glow underneath your pillow. Visualize its powers to comfort you and ease you off any emotional pains or stress. Communicate to your crystal and tell it to help you and comfort you.

Chapter Seven: Other Purposes of Crystals

Step #4: Take deep breaths as you imagine yourself absorbing the comforting energies being emitted from your crystal. Imagine that the glow emanating from your stone is growing wider underneath your pillow. Visualize that the powerful energy is flowing in your head and freeing you from any negative thoughts. The glow will then spread throughout your entire body, enveloping you as you take a rest.

Step #5: As you visualize that your crystal's power is spreading throughout your body, you can start shifting into sleeping position and know that your gem will do its wonders as you sleep. If you find yourself falling as sleep as you visualize, it's perfectly fine as it means that you are absorbing the comforting energies of the stone. If you find yourself still awake, just continue to do your visualization and try to feel the comforting energy surrounding you. You might start to notice that you feel more at ease and light when you wake up the next day and this is because the negative thoughts have been removed from you and you allow yourself to receive comfort.

Chapter Seven: Other Purposes of Crystals

Step #6: As you get up from a good night sleep, take your stone underneath your pillow and give thanks to it. You can then cleanse it under the morning sun to recharge the crystal.

How to Keep Creative Ideas Flowing

If you want to have creativity flowing through you, what you need to do is to just place any of the stones below in your work area or wherever you need a dose of inspiration and continuous spark of ideas. You can also combine these crystals, and follow your intuition when it comes to putting your stone/s in the right places.

- Alexandrite
- Milky Quartz
- Tourmaline
- Citrine
- Garnet

Chapter Seven: Other Purposes of Crystals

How to Find Inspiration

The method below will help you in finding inspiration. If you apply this technique, inspiration can come from different forms so make sure to keep an open mind and just let the ideas flow through you until you find the right ones. Do this whenever you are experiencing lack of ideas or inspiration.

Prepare the following items:

- Yellow or coffee – scented candle
- Candle holder or fireproof dish
- Pad paper and pen
- Any of these stones:
    - Alexandrite
    - Citrine
    - Tourmaline
    - Aventurine
    - Green Tourmaline
    - Aquamarine

Chapter Seven: Other Purposes of Crystals

Instructions:

Step #1: Find a quiet spot where you won't be disturbed. If you're doing the ritual during the day, make sure to close the windows/ curtains to prevent too much light on the inside. On the other hand, if you're doing it during the night, make sure that you put on dim lights.

Step #2: Bring all the materials you need with you. Sit down and meditate by closing your eyes, taking deep breaths, and relaxing your body. Try to be at peace and empty your mind.

Step #3: Open your eyes whenever you're ready to start. Place the candle on the holder or fireproof dish and keep it near you together with your pad paper and pen.

Step #4: Pick up your crystal with both hands and close your eyes. Communicate with your stone using your mind and ask for the inspiration you seek. Once you ask for inspiration, trust that your stone will help you in bringing it to you. Let go of any worrisome thoughts so that the inspiration you need will have a space in your mind and you'll be ready to receive it.

Chapter Seven: Other Purposes of Crystals

Step #5: Open your eyes and then put your crystal on a blank piece of your pad paper. By doing this, you are sort of lifting up your concern to the Universe using the powers and energy within your stone.

Step #6: After doing this, the next thing you need to do is to continuously empty your mind as you lay your eyes on the candle flame, and do this as long as necessary. During this period, ideas may rush to you that's given by the Universe itself when this happens, make sure to capture it by being mindful and writing it down on your pad paper. You'll soon notice that you already have written a handful of ideas and concepts. Thank your stone after using it and cleanse it to recharge its energies.

Crystals for Empowering Yourself with Positive Energy

The methods we've taught you pretty much involve getting rid of negative energies so that you can open and allow yourself for positive energies to come in. If you find it effective, know that it's not just because of the power contained in your stones but also your own positive energy.

Chapter Seven: Other Purposes of Crystals

In addition from attracting wealth, inspiration, love, healing and emotional ease, there are other methods that you can use to further enhance the positive energy within you and your gemstones. This section will teach you how to use your crystals to empower the beauty, happiness, and confidence that's already within you, and how to sustain these energies.

Using Crystals to Live Each Day in Happiness

This technique will teach you how you can use certain crystals to not just magnify your inner and outer beauty but to also multiply your happiness. If you're truly happy inside, your beauty will naturally come out. Keep in mind though that your crystal doesn't make you happy or beautiful because it's already within you, these stones just help you magnify what you already have and let your inner happiness radiate through you.

Chapter Seven: Other Purposes of Crystals

Prepare any of the following items:

- Sapphire
- Rose Quartz
- Purple Jade
- Amber
- Crazy Lace Agate

Instructions:

Step #1: Allow your crystal to bathe under the moon overnight before you proceed in doing this practice.

Step #2: When you finally wake up the following day, pick up the cleansed crystal and hold it in your palms. Communicate with it by greeting it and giving thanks for a new day ahead so that your crystal will be charge with gratitude vibes and positive energies.

Step #3: Tell yourself that today will be a great day, and as you do this make sure to smile and stretch your arms while you're holding your crystal. When you already felt that the stone is charged with blissful feelings, you can then place it near the spot where you get ready for the day.

Chapter Seven: Other Purposes of Crystals

Step #4: As you start your day, be mindful that your crystal is doing its work through magnifying your inner beauty and happiness. Feel the feelings of joy and positivity that your stone is emanating.

Step #5: Before you leave for work, pick up your crystal and close your eyes for a moment. Hold the stone close to your heart and say something like "I am surrounded by beauty, kindness, and happiness." Open your eyes and carry the stone with you throughout the day.

Step #6: As you go through your day, you can touch or rub the stone from time to time so that you would feel its comforting power. Be mindful of how the stone is working through you making you more beautiful and radiant to the people around you.

Step #7: If ever you felt a little tired or you have a need to boost your energy, you can just close your eyes while you're holding the crystal. Communicate with it and ask for its help so that you can tap into its energy and empower the strength that's within you.

Chapter Seven: Other Purposes of Crystals

Step #8: At the end of the day, cleanse the stone by leaving it overnight under the moonlight. Do the same steps the next day for as long as you feel is necessary.

Using Crystals to Increase the Flow of Good Luck

Carry or wear these gems to attract good luck into your life. The crystals below are known to contain powerful energies that will invite good luck to anyone who bears them.

- Black Tourmaline
- Aventurine
- Alexandrite
- Amber
- Turquoise

Cleansing a Room or Space of Negative Energy

The method below involves actual cleaning of the room or space that has some form of negative energy. It's

Chapter Seven: Other Purposes of Crystals

best to do this method during spring – cleaning or whenever you feel like cleaning up. Don't do this method if you feel like you're being forced or obliged to do so. It's important that when you do this technique you are happy or enjoying the activity because if not, you could release more negative energy into the room. For this method, you'll need to prepare a cluster of quartz crystal or a large piece of Amethyst. The instructions below are quite easy and simple to do though it would take some time depending on the size of the room and the amount of cleaning needed.

Instructions:

Step #1: Start cleaning your room and make sure to open the windows. Burn an incense with Eucalyptus, Sandalwood, or Cinnamon scent as it helps in increasing the flow of cleansing energies. Make sure to get rid of all the clutter and change the curtains & sheets if necessary.

Step #2: After you have thoroughly clean the room, place the cluster of Quartz Crystal or the piece of Amethyst upon the bed (if any). Leave the stone there so that it can absorb all the negative energies in the room including the scattered

Chapter Seven: Other Purposes of Crystals

energies due to you cleaning up. If things are thrown out, moved or cleaned it can cause energies to be scattered.

Step #3: Once you feel that the stones have absorbed all the negative energy in the room, you can now cleanse it using any of the following methods we discussed earlier in this book before placing it back on its container. Repeat this process especially when you feel that a room is filled with stale or heavy energy.

Step #4: It's also ideal to place an amethyst or clusters of quartz crystal on hotel beds so that you can cleanse the room from any negative energy left behind by the previous guests. Obviously, you won't have to do any general cleaning since hotel rooms are usually clean before you come in. Doing this method can help you have a peaceful sleep even if you're not in your own room. Leaving an amethyst or quartz crystal on the bed while you're off to a meeting or something is also ideal so that the room is already cleansed when you get ready for bed.

Chapter Seven: Other Purposes of Crystals

Improving the Flow of Energy within Your Home

Quartz crystal can definitely help you in improving the flow of energy at home particularly if you have a staircase. It's ideal to place a quartz crystal on each step of your staircase. Placing crystals in your home can definitely help in attracting positive, happy and light energies. You can also places smaller pieces of quartz crystals between openings in the house. If you choose to do this, then make sure that the points of the quartz crystal are facing in a downward direction.

Crystals for Protection

Certain crystal and gems have protective energies that can shield a person from negative, stale, or heavy energies. There are also stones that can banish negativity and prevent an individual from being affected by it. Most of these protective crystals and gems are carried or worn as an amulet. Here is a list of crystals that you can carry or wear wherever you go:

- Jade
- Citrine
- Ruby
- Black Tourmaline

Chapter Seven: Other Purposes of Crystals

- Smoky Quartz
- Garnet
- Turquoise
- Agate
- Emerald
- Blue Fluorite
- Quartz Crystal

After attuning and cleansing the protective crystals and gems, it's ideal to meditate with your stones while imagining that its powers are creating a shield and protecting you from harmful energies. Meditation strengthens your bond with these crystals and enhances their protective powers especially when you carry or wear them.

Chapter Seven: Other Purposes of Crystals

Photo Credits

Introduction Page Photo by user Alosyius via Pixabay.com,

https://pixabay.com/en/gems-stones-crystal-gemstone-836763/

Page 2 Photo by user Brett - Hondow via Pixabay.com,

https://pixabay.com/en/gems-gemstones-semi-precious-stones-1400677/

Page 10 Photo by user Bogomir Bogomirov via Flickr.com,

https://www.flickr.com/photos/bogomirov/6261069204/

Page 21 Photo by user Outi via Flickr.com,

https://www.flickr.com/photos/helmetti/513372290/

Page 35 Photo by user alusruvi via Pixabay.com,

https://pixabay.com/en/rock-crystal-clear-to-white-gem-top-1603474/

Page 62 Photo by user Clker - Free - Vector - Images via Pixabay.com,

https://pixabay.com/en/stones-ruby-emerald-garnet-topaz-36744/

Page 83 Photo by user TessaMannonen via Pixabay.com,

https://pixabay.com/en/crystals-stones-healing-mystic-1567953/

Page 102 Photo by user PublicDomainPictures via Pixabay.com,

https://pixabay.com/en/diamond-black-rich-brilliant-316610/

References

The Magical Power of Gemstones and Crystals - Tanahoy.com

http://www.tanahoy.com/wp-content/uploads/2011/05/Proofread-Gemstones-book-copy.pdf

A Beginner's Guide to Healing Crystals - EnergyMuse.com

https://www.energymuse.com/blog/wp-content/uploads/2017/04/A-Beginners-uide-to-Healing-Crystals.pdf

Crystal Healing: The Ultimate Beginner's Guide to Crystal Healing - New Horizon Preston

http://newhorizonzpreston.com/publications/crystalhealing.pdf

Crystals For Beginners! Here Are the Top 10 Essential Crystals & Their Uses - Collective - Evolution.com

https://www.collective-evolution.com/2017/02/12/crystals-for-beginners-here-are-the-top-10-essential-crystals/

About Gemstones - EnergyMuse.com

https://www.energymuse.com/about-gemstones

Crystal A - Z - HappyGlastonBury.co.uk

https://www.happyglastonbury.co.uk/product-category/crystals/crystal-a-z/

The Secrets of Crystal Healing: A Complete Guide to Supercharging the Mind, Body and Spirit with Sacred Stones and Minerals - Conscious Lifestyle Magazine

https://www.consciouslifestylemag.com/crystal-healing-guide/

There's a Crystal For That: A Highly Specific Guide - Bon Appetit

https://www.bonappetit.com/gallery/beginners-guide-to-crystals

A Room-By-Room Guide to Using Crystals for The Home - EnergyMuse.com

https://www.energymuse.com/blog/using-crystals-for-the-home-and-interior-design/

Where to Put Your Crystals In Your Home For Maximum Good Energy Vibes - Pedestrian.tv

https://www.pedestrian.tv/home/where-to-put-crystals-in-your-home/

www.ingramcontent.com/pod-product-compliance
Lightning Source LLC
LaVergne TN
LVHW051841080426
835512LV00018B/2998